THE CHANGING FACE OF
CANADA

Text by CATHERINE and D'ARCY LITTLE
Photographs by CHRIS FAIRCLOUGH

HODDER
Wayland

an imprint of Hodder Children's Books

© 2002 White-Thomson Publishing Ltd

Produced for Hodder Wayland by
White-Thomson Publishing Ltd
2/3 St Andrew's Place
Lewes BN7 1UP

Editor: Alison Cooper
Designer: Christopher Halls at Mind's Eye Design, Lewes
Proofreader: Philippa Smith
Additional picture research: Shelley Noronha, Glass Onion Pictures

First published in Great Britain in 2002 by Hodder Wayland, an imprint
of Hodder Children's Books.
This paperback edition published in 2004

British Library Cataloguing in Publication Data
Little, Catherine
  Changing Face of Canada
  1. Canada - Juvenile literature
  I. Title II. Little, D'Arcy III. Cooper, Alison, 1967- IV. Canada
  971
ISBN: 0 7502 3999 9

Printed in China

Hodder Children's Books
A division of Hodder Headline Limited,
338 Euston Rd, London NW1 3BH

Acknowledgements
The publishers would like to thank
the following: Rob Bowden – statistics
panel research; Peter Bull – map
illustration; Nick Hawken – statistics
panel illustrations. All photographs are
by Chris Fairclough except: Bryan and
Cherry Alexander 10, 27 (lower);
James Davis Travel Photography 7;
Popperfoto 13 (top), 26.

Contents

Toronto – a Meeting Place

The Hurons, a native North American people, named a favourite spot on the shore of Lake Ontario 'To'ron'to', which means 'Place of Meeting'. Over several hundred years Toronto, now the largest city in Canada, has lived up to its name. It has become a city that people of many nations have made their home. The United Nations has declared Toronto to be the most multiculturally diverse city in the world. People come to Toronto for many different reasons, but often they are attracted by the promise of a better life.

Visiting the different neighbourhoods of Toronto can feel like taking a tour of the world. The shops, street signs and languages spoken reflect the many different ethnic communities that make up the city's population. In most cases, people of different religions and ethnic backgrounds live in harmony and enjoy learning from one another. Dragon Boat Races, for example, are a tradition that belonged originally to the Chinese community. Now teams representing a range of businesses and community groups compete and celebrate together, in races that take place each year around Toronto's Centre Island.

▲ *The Canadian National Tower is Toronto's most famous landmark.*

▼ *The population of Toronto is the most diverse in the world.*

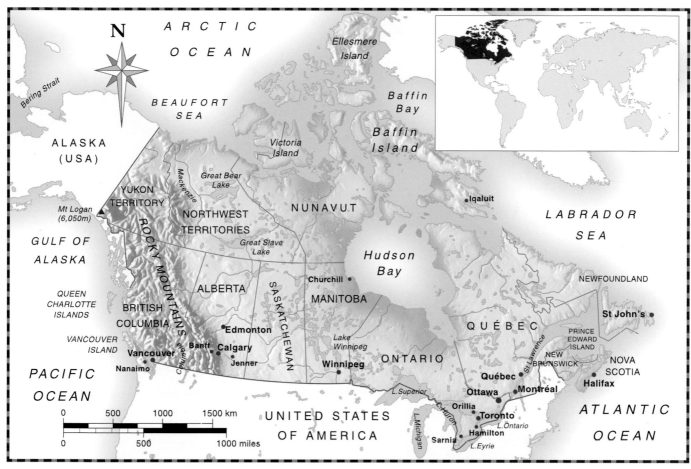

▲ *This map shows Canada's major towns and cities, as well as the main landscape features and places mentioned in this book.*

CANADA: KEY FACTS

Area: 9,970,610 sq km

Population: 30,750,087

Population density: 3.1 people per square km (1999); population is concentrated close to the southern border

Capital city: Ottawa (1,065,021)

Other main cities: Toronto (4,680,250), Montréal (3,438,532), Vancouver (2,016,643), Calgary (933,748), Winnipeg (677,625)

Highest mountain: Mount Logan (6,050 m)

Longest river: Mackenzie (4,241 km)

Main languages: English and French share status as official languages

Major religions: Catholicism (45%), United Church (12%), Anglicanism (8%). Other religions include Judaism, Islam, Hinduism, Sikhism and Buddhism

Currency: Canadian dollar (100 cents = 1 dollar)

2 Past Times

Canada's human history begins with the native peoples who are thought to have travelled to Canada from Asia in ancient times. They were able to cross into Canada because the continents were linked by a 'bridge' of land in the area that is now the Bering Strait. They made homes all across Canada and lived there for over 12,000 years before the first Europeans arrived.

European settlement

Viking ships reached the eastern shores of Canada around CE 1000, but Europeans did not make permanent settlements until the sixteenth century. French and British explorers realized that they could make good profits by trading furs with the native peoples. In 1541, Jacques Cartier and Sieur de Roberval founded the first French settlement in America and named it Charlesbourg-Royal. Soon, the immediate area became known as 'New France'. In the seventeenth and early eighteenth centuries the French and British fought each other for control of Canada. The territory finally came under British control in 1763.

In 1867, the British North America Act was passed and Canada became a dominion in the British Empire. The British monarch is still head of state in Canada but the Canadian Parliament is free to make its own laws and change the country's constitution.

▶ *A carved wooden totem pole. Totem poles are traditional symbols used by the native Canadians.*

IN THEIR OWN WORDS

'Hi, my name is Aimee Greenaway and I'm an elementary school teacher in Nanaimo on Vancouver Island. At the weekends I dress up in Victorian costume and work as a tourist guide at our local landmark, the Bastion. The Bastion is a wooden fort, built in 1853 to protect a coal mine set up by European settlers. It was equipped with cannons, just in case the fort was ever attacked by native Canadians who wanted to reclaim their territory. The cannons probably get more use now than they did in the old days though – we fire them every day as a way of welcoming visitors to Nanaimo. You can see me in this picture, in the flowery red dress (right), getting ready to fire the cannon.'

Québec

The French influence on Canada's history has not been forgotten. Today, the area originally named 'New France' is known as Québec and French is its official language. Some of the people who live in Québec feel that their French language and culture would be better protected if Québec were to separate from Canada and run its own affairs. In referendums the people of Québec have so far voted to remain part of Canada but the votes have sometimes been very close. The debate over Québec's future has caused disagreements throughout the country.

▶ *The French influence on Québec can be seen in its street signs and the style of its buildings.*

3 Landscape and Climate

Canada is the second-largest country in the world after Russia. It shares the longest undefended border in the world with the USA, not only in the south but also in the north-west, where Canada borders the US state of Alaska. Because of its immense area, it is no surprise that the natural landscape is very varied, including tundra, forest and grassland. The Pacific, Atlantic and Arctic Oceans border the country to the west, east and north. Mountain ranges, including the Rocky Mountains in the west, add drama to the landscape.

▲ People enjoy canoeing on Lake Louise in Banff National Park, in the Rocky Mountains.

◄ Vancouver is the main seaport on Canada's Pacific coast. Its harbour remains ice-free all year round.

British Columbia

British Columbia, the westernmost province, is one of the most picturesque areas in Canada. Three mountain ranges, the Coast Mountains, the Columbia Mountains and the Rocky Mountains, run down the length of the province. The Pacific Ocean influences its climate, giving it the most moderate weather in the country. This allows farmers to cultivate a variety of fruits, including apples, cherries, peaches, pears, plums and grapes, in places like the Okanagan Valley. The average temperature in Vancouver in the month of July is 21.7 °C and in January it is 3 °C. The annual total precipitation of Vancouver is very high at 1,167 mm.

IN THEIR OWN WORDS

'I'm Herdev Sanserwal and I own this apple orchard outside Vancouver. I came here from the Punjab thirteen years ago when my sister and her husband sponsored me. At first I worked in the timber industry, but the work wasn't interesting, so after a few years I leased 120 hectares of land from a farmer here in the Okanagan Valley and decided to grow apples. Now I employ up to ten people and produce 1,500 bins of apples each year. One of the biggest adjustments I had to make was to the weather. I'd never seen snow and it was really cold for the first few years! Now I'm used to it and I've even bought a small snowmobile to get around the orchard.'

The east coast

On the other side of Canada, the Atlantic provinces have a different feel from some of the other provinces. Although there are some major cities, they are not as large as the ones to the west. The landscape tends towards rolling hills, with reddish soil. The summer temperature of Halifax, Nova Scotia, averages 17.5 °C and the winter averages –4.6 °C.

Tundra

The tundra region in the far north of Canada is like a frozen desert. It is cold and dry with less than 250 mm of precipitation per year. In winter it is covered in snow and ice. In summer the top layer of soil thaws but the lower layers stay frozen all year round. Low-growing plants carpet the boggy ground but no trees can grow here.

▲ *Snow covers the tundra and the sea is frozen here in Nunavut, in the far north of Canada.*

Forests

Boreal forest forms a belt from Newfoundland in the east to the Rockies in the west and is Canada's largest forest region. Boreal forest consists mainly of evergreen trees. Temperate forest covers a smaller area of the country. This region receives much more precipitation than the boreal forest region and temperate forest is mainly made up of deciduous trees. These provide a spectacular display every autumn when the leaves turn from green to gold, orange and yellow.

IN THEIR OWN WORDS

'I'm Randy Axani and I work as a conservation officer with the Alberta Forest Service. I look after the trails and paths that lead through the mountains and forests, issue permits for walkers and campers, do mountain rescue, teach climbing and even deal with the occasional grizzly bear. When bears get too close to the public, we trap them and take them back into the forest for their own good and to protect the people. Lack of rain is a big worry for us. When the forests are really dry there is an increased risk of fire so we have to ban camp fires and educate the public about how to avoid starting fires.'

The prairies

The flat prairie provinces of Alberta, Saskatchewan and Manitoba are located in the middle of Canada. This area has some of the most severe weather in the country. Although summer temperatures are often in the mid-thirties (degrees Celsius), in winter temperatures fall as low as 40° below freezing. The natural vegetation of the region is grassland, and the climate and rich, brown soil are ideal for growing wheat. In the late 1800s, the Canadian government advertised in regions such as the Ukraine for Europeans to come and farm this area of the country. It has been Canada's main wheat-growing area ever since.

▼ *A combine harvester at work near Calgary in Alberta. The flat, open plains make it easy to use large machines like this.*

Climate change

Scientists who study climate change believe that Canada may experience more noticeable warming than other countries closer to the equator. While the global average increase in temperature over the last hundred years has been 2 °C, Canada has experienced double this increase. Rises in sea-level could lead to flooding and erosion in low-lying coastal areas, such as the highly-populated Fraser River delta in the west and Prince Edward Island, Halifax and St John's in the east. In the prairies, higher temperatures could bring more frequent periods of drought. In the Great Lakes region, warmer summers could increase water evaporation, causing water levels in the Great Lakes to drop by almost one metre.

◄ *This river in Alberta is lower than it has ever been in living memory. You can see the dry river bed at the top of the picture.*

In the far north, global warming threatens the survival of the polar bear. The bears travel widely across the ice in their search for food but records show that areas of the Arctic are remaining ice-free for longer. This makes it more difficult for the bears to hunt. People who live in isolated communities often rely on being able to travel across the ice, too. Warmer temperatures in the tundra region may make these communities even more isolated.

Freak weather?

Unusually severe weather conditions have made headlines in the news in recent years. In 1997 the Red River region of the prairies experienced a flood that some described as the worst in a lifetime. A severe ice storm wreaked havoc in eastern Ontario and Québec in 1998. Ice froze on power lines and the weight of the ice eventually caused the lines to collapse, cutting power to thousands of homes. Some scientists believe that unusual weather events like this are a result of climate change.

▲ *A power worker struggles to restore an electricity supply to a farm near Ottawa, Ontario, following the 1998 ice storm.*

IN THEIR OWN WORDS

'I'm Stan Krause. With my wife Robin I work 43,000 hectares of some of the driest land on the planet here at Jenner, Alberta. We've been managing an average of 500 head of cattle since the 1970s when we bought this ranch from my parents. Our two children have grown up and left but Robin and I will probably stay for the rest of our days. A life like this, away from the noise and bustle of modern living, gets in your blood – I wouldn't know what else to do after a lifetime here in the flat lands! Our major worry is water. Water levels are the lowest they have been in thirty years. Next year, they are predicting no rain at all – and the same for the next few years. If that prediction comes true, it will be a real disaster!'

Natural Resources

Canada's natural resources fall into three broad categories – minerals, energy and forestry. Together, they make up over 11 per cent of the gross domestic product. Canada produces over 60 minerals and metals, owns 10 per cent of the world's forests and exports 30 billion dollars' worth of energy-related products yearly. Over 90 per cent of these exports go to the USA.

Energy production

Affordable and reliable energy is especially important to Canada. The great distances between cities make transport costs high and the long, cold winters make it essential to use domestic heating and lighting for long periods. The country is rich in supplies of oil, natural gas, coal and uranium and some rivers have been dammed so that hydroelectricity can be produced. The demand for energy continues to increase and the way the energy is produced is changing. The proportion of energy generated by oil, coal, hydroelectricity, nuclear energy, steam and biomass has dropped since the mid-1980s and reliance on natural gas has increased.

▲ The Revelstoke dam on the Columbia River is used in the generation of hydroelectricity. The reservoir behind the 175-m high dam is 130 km long.

◀ Most of Canada's oil and natural gas supplies come from plants like this one in Alberta. People who live in Alberta get their fuel cheaper than people living further away from the gas fields.

Oil production from the Hibernia field, off the coast of Newfoundland, is an important new development. The Hibernia oil platform is a massive structure, designed to withstand the impact of icebergs, and more than 185 people live and work there. It began producing oil from deep beneath the sea-bed in 1997 and it has a maximum capacity of 150,000 barrels of crude oil per day.

▶ *Canada is exploring alternative energy sources. A wind turbine has been built alongside the nuclear power station in Pickering, Ontario.*

IN THEIR OWN WORDS

'Hi, we're Kevin and Rob and we're 15. We study the risks and benefits of nuclear power in school and feel that it's important to explore alternative ways to generate electricity. Pickering is well known for its nuclear power plant but we've come here today to look at the wind turbine. The power lines you can see behind us carry electricity generated by both the nuclear plant and the wind turbine. It's an impressive project but we've found out that only 1 per cent of Canada's energy needs is supplied by wind power. We hope more work will be done on developing alternative energy sources.'

Mining

Both base metals, such as zinc, copper, lead and nickel, and precious metals, such as gold, silver and platinum, are mined in Canada. Diamond mines in the Northwest Territories may eventually supply more than 5 per cent of the world's production. The Canadian mining industry is a world leader in the use of electronics and telecommunications. Women as well as men work as miners; there has been a Women's Association of Mining in Canada since the 1920s.

Forests

Forests have played an important role in the Canadian economy since the arrival of the Europeans. Explorers found the forests teeming with beaver, and the furs were exported to supply European markets. Timber, which has been used to build houses for thousands of years by Canada's native peoples, is now an important export. Wood pulp is used to make paper. On a smaller scale, maple syrup (which is made by boiling the sap of maple trees) and its by-products, such as sugar and candy, are often associated with Canada.

◀ This forester on Vancouver Island is taking a sample from a tree to check for disease.

IN THEIR OWN WORDS

'Hi, I'm Travis McLean. I'm 17 and I've been working as a guide taking tourists salmon fishing. My grandfather was a whaler out of Ucluelet and Dad was a longliner till the fishing over here on the west coast of Vancouver Island got real bad, about 15 years ago. The seas were over-fished and now the industry hardly exists. My work with the tourists is seasonal so during the off season I live back in Nanaimo and labour on building sites. I think there's a real opportunity with tourism – there's some great scenery and fascinating wildlife out here. We get lots of folks looking for whales, wanting to fish or just sightseeing. I think there's a great future for me.'

Processed products

In the past, Canada exported its natural resources such as fish, wheat, metals and coal as raw materials to markets across the world. Now, most natural resources are processed in Canada before export. Fish are smoked and packaged. Trees are shipped as shingles, lumber or pulp and paper products. Canada's main trading partner is the United States, although trade with Japan and the European Union is also important to the Canadian economy.

▲ *Traditional log cabins like these are produced for export. The cabins are put together, the pieces are numbered and then they are taken down and packed for shipping. Many go to Japan.*

5 The Changing Environment

Canada has scored consistently high in United Nations' studies, which often rank Canada as the best place in the world to live. Despite this, Canada does have problems linked to pollution. Many of these are worst in urban areas where dense populations exist.

Traffic problems

City streets are becoming more and more crowded with cars. Since housing prices are usually higher in the cities than in the surrounding suburbs, large numbers of workers choose to live outside the city centres. Many people drive for an hour or more each day to get to work in the city. The large number of cars is a great source of frustration to drivers and is a significant cause of pollution.

Sometimes, 'smog alerts' warn residents with breathing difficulties to stay indoors. Smog alerts happen most frequently during the hot, humid days of summer. In large urban areas, the pollution from car exhausts reacts with light from the sun to produce a brown, smelly photochemical smog. For most people the smog is unpleasant, but for the elderly and those with illnesses such as asthma it can have devastating health consequences.

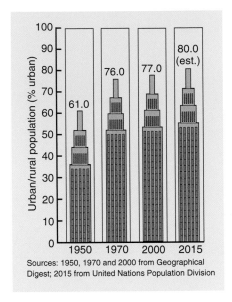

Sources: 1950, 1970 and 2000 from Geographical Digest; 2015 from United Nations Population Division

▲ More than three-quarters of Canada's population now live in urban areas.

▼ With more people living or working in the cities the amount of traffic on the cities' roads has increased.

Water pollution

People enjoy water sports on Canada's Great Lakes and the region is also the source of drinking water for millions. Yet 45 per cent of Canada's industries are located in the Great Lakes region, the water is used by power stations, and large cargo ships use the ports around the lakes. Discharges from industry have caused major pollution problems. Sewage overflows are a problem that is getting worse as city populations increase. When large amounts of water drain into the sewers after heavy rains they overflow, and untreated sewage enters the lakes. Beaches around the lakes have to be closed because of the danger to people's health.

▶ *Chemical pollution from industry is a concern in the Great Lakes.*

IN THEIR OWN WORDS

'Hi, we are Kathleen and Kerri-Lee. We enjoy swimming, jet-skiing and tubing here at our family cottage on Lake Dalrymple. Tubing is great – we sit in a big inner tube and get pulled along by a motor boat. Jet-skiing and tubing are pretty noisy though and not everyone round here is keen on them. Today, we're going out with Dad on our boat to do some quiet fishing! We enjoy the clean air and water away from our city home. Water in the city lakes is not as nice to swim in and the air in the country seems to be easier to breathe. It would be great to be able to live here all year round, but Mum and Dad's work keeps us all in the city.'

Tackling the problems

The Great Lakes Water Quality Agreements are an environmental initiative between the province of Ontario in Canada and the United States. The aim is to improve the quality of the water in the Great Lakes, by regulating the amount of waste products that industries can release into the lakes, and by agreeing standards of wastewater treatment. The people of Toronto, Hamilton and Sarnia have benefited greatly from these agreements. Canada has also participated in global initiatives to improve the environment. In June 1986, it became the first nation to ratify the Vienna Convention for the protection of the ozone layer.

◄ *Making greater use of the public transport system is one way to cut down on pollution.*

Transport initiatives

Large urban areas are tackling the problems of pollution in a number of ways. One approach is through the development of public transport. Underground subway systems, light rail transit systems and extensive bus routes exist in major cities. This helps to ease traffic congestion as well as cutting down on air pollution. However, many transport commissions are experiencing financial difficulties due to changes in government funding. They are seeking changes that will help them to replace ageing machinery and expand routes.

IN THEIR OWN WORDS

'I'm Barbara Titherington. I am a mental health nurse at a community health centre. I am also very interested in the environment so I completed a further degree in environmental studies in my spare time. As part of my job at the health centre I started a community garden in 1991. This project allows many different people, some with illnesses, to work together. They grow their own organic vegetables, share their knowledge, and develop an understanding of how important it is to take good care of the land.

'I think that the community garden movement is important in the promotion of healthy cities. Many of the people who are involved in the community garden do other things to protect the environment, such as recycling their rubbish and travelling by public transport or bicycles.'

In some cities, lanes reserved for cyclists on the road are gaining in popularity. This initiative works well in cities like Vancouver, where the mild weather encourages people to ride their bicycles for most of the year, but in cities like Montréal the harsh winter weather will keep even the most dedicated environmentalist off the road.

▶ *Recycling schemes reduce the amount of household waste that has to be sent to landfill sites. Bales of waste paper from this collection point are sent over the border to a recycling plant in the USA.*

6

The Changing Population

Population diversity

Although Canada's first immigrants were the French and the British, information from the 1996 census shows that only half of Canada's present population has either of these ethnic backgrounds. Today's Canadians may just as easily have family roots in Africa, Asia or South America. Canada's population includes people from over 160 different countries. Community groups to preserve culture, language and traditions are encouraged and their special events are enjoyed by the wider public. Canadians have learned to value and appreciate the diversity of their population.

Immigration policies

Canada has always been a country of immigrants, starting with the French and the British. In the beginning, immigration was the only way to populate such a vast country. Immigration has also been used to fill jobs. For example, when nurses were needed, or workers for the manufacturing and building industries, immigrants with those skills were preferred. Immigration has also been permitted to allow family members from abroad to join their relatives already living in Canada.

▲ *An Islamic centre and a Portuguese supermarket, side by side in a district of Toronto.*

Changes ahead?

Recently, however, there have been calls to change Canada's immigration and refugee policies. Critics of the existing policies have called for reforms to ensure that only law-abiding immigrants are welcomed. They want decisions to be made more quickly when people ask to be allowed to stay in Canada as refugees. There have also been calls for Canada to give preference to immigrants who are highly skilled. Many people find it hard to decide on this issue, because so many have benefited from Canada's immigration policies in the past. If such changes are brought in, other families like theirs will not have the opportunity to make a new life in the country.

▶ *The French influence on Canada is seen in signs like this, where visitors to a national park are warned in French and English to beware of a rogue bear.*

IN THEIR OWN WORDS

'Hi, I'm Arron Eisen and this is my family. Debbie used to live in the USA but moved to Canada when she was an adult. We met and married in our forties so when we decided we wanted a family we adopted Samantha from China. She was 17 months old when we went to Changsha in Hunan province to bring her home. We and fifteen other families were helped by an agency that organizes the adoption of children from foreign countries. Toronto is the perfect place for us because it is so ethnically diverse. We can teach Samantha about Chinese culture and she can attend Jewish day school to learn about ours.'

Population growth

Canada welcomes hundreds of thousands of people from all over the world every year and this is an important factor in population growth. New immigrants choose Canada for the opportunities that exist and also because it is easy for them to feel at home. With such a variety of ethnic groups already living in Canada, it is usually possible for new immigrants to find familiar newspapers, foods and radio and television programmes. Increased life expectancy is another important factor in population growth. Presently, the life expectancy for men is over 74 years; for women it is over 80 years.

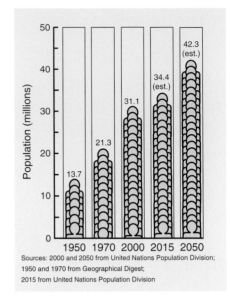

Sources: 2000 and 2050 from United Nations Population Division;
1950 and 1970 from Geographical Digest;
2015 from United Nations Population Division

▲ *Canada's population more than doubled in the second half of the twentieth century.*

An ageing population

As a result of increased life expectancy, today's seniors can look forward to many healthy years after the standard retirement age of 65. Currently, seniors make up over 12 per cent of the population – up from just over 7 per cent in the 1960s. The proportion of seniors to the rest of the population is expected to continue to grow as life expectancy increases. The needs of the elderly population have to be taken into account when planning housing, access to facilities, services such as home helps, and the market for consumer goods.

▶ *A hoarding advertising a new housing development, built especially for seniors. Many retired people in Canada are quite well off and can afford a good standard of living.*

IN THEIR OWN WORDS

'I'm Sybil Langman and I was born in 1909 in a small community called Chapleau in Ontario. Over my life, I've lived and travelled all across Canada. I've lived in big cities like Toronto and isolated northern communities. When I was younger, I enjoyed the hustle and bustle of big city life with its people and places to go. The last time I visited Toronto, I noticed lots more people and cars than I remembered. It was hard to get around and everyone was in a hurry. Now that I'm older, I prefer a quieter, smaller city like Orillia. I have my own apartment in a retirement home and don't have to worry about buying groceries or preparing meals. We have outings and my family visits me regularly. I like it here.'

The growing cities

In the 1930s about 54 per cent of Canada's population lived in cities while 46 per cent lived in the country. Of those people who lived in the country, 31 per cent lived on farms. Today almost 80 per cent of the population live in cities. Of those living in the country, only around 3 per cent still live on farms. City populations have increased because people have moved from the countryside to the cities and also because most new immigrants settle in large cities. This dramatic shift in population has created many problems. In the cities it has led to overcrowding, increased pollution and a high cost of living. In rural areas traditional farming skills are disappearing.

▲ *An abandoned farmhouse in Alberta. The land around here has become too dry and lacking in nutrients to grow crops and the farmers have moved away.*

Life in the north

Before European settlers arrived, parts of Canada were occupied by native Canadian peoples. One of the issues Canada has to deal with today are the demands by native Canadians for more rights over the land that was once theirs. In 1999, one group of people, the Inuit, won the right to govern themselves. The eastern part of the Northwest Territories became 'Nunavut' – the name is Inuktitut for 'our land'.

With the settlement came $1.1 billion to be paid in instalments, over 356,000 sq km of land and all of the rights and responsibilities to go with it. Among the challenges that face the new provincial government is the high cost of goods and services – the cost of transporting goods to this remote area makes everything expensive. It also has to deal with a young and inexperienced workforce, high unemployment and a poor level of education.

▼ *These Inuit men in Iqaluit are producing traditional carvings that will be sold to tourists.*

IN THEIR OWN WORDS

'I'm Donald Buckle and I live in Halifax, Nova Scotia. Right now, though, I'm on my way up to Churchill, on the coast of Hudson Bay. I work there all through the summer, on a tug that guides in the big barges bringing fuel supplies. In winter the bay freezes over and the fuel has to be brought in over the ice by truck. Planes fly in with lighter stuff like food or passengers, providing the weather is OK.

'Churchill used to be a really quiet place but a lot of tourists go up there now – it's a great place to see the polar bears. Me, I prefer to see them from a good long distance – when I'm safely on my tug, for instance.'

The federal government is involved in many programmes to boost the economy. Tourism is providing new jobs, with Inuit acting as guides to tourists who want to see the unspoiled wilderness of the far north for themselves. The sale of arts and crafts boosts the economy and helps traditional skills to survive. Developments in telecommunications and information technology, such as the internet, offer the potential for a wider range of work, but people first need to gain new skills, so that they can take advantage of new opportunities.

▼ *A polar bear investigates a tourist buggy near Churchill in Manitoba. 'Eco-tourism' is an important source of income for communities in the far north.*

7

Changes at Home

Family life

Family life in Canada is very diverse. As well as the 'traditional' family unit of a mother, father and children, there are many single-parent families and extended families with several generations living under the same roof. There are also many couples who cannot have or choose not to have children. The average number of children per family is decreasing. In 2001 the national average was 3.0, down from 3.7 in 1971.

Childcare

A major concern facing many families is the issue of childcare. Who will take care of the children if both parents go out to work or if there is only one parent? The majority of single-parent families are headed by women. Often, they do not have family support and cannot afford the costs of daycare or a baby-sitter. The government does provide some

◄ *Approximately 15 per cent of Canadian families are headed by a single parent, usually a mother.*

IN THEIR OWN WORDS

'Hi, I'm Lily Law Jutlah. I was born in Hong Kong but came to Canada when I was 3. My husband, Brian, was born and raised in Canada but his family is originally from Trinidad. When we decided to get married, race was not an issue for us in the way it was for our neighbours. They were married over 25 years ago, when it was uncommon to marry someone of a different culture, and their families didn't accept their choices very well.

'However, Brian and I find that we have plenty in common so our biggest issue is how to balance home and work life. Brian is a dentist and I run my own urban planning firm. We are lucky to have our parents living nearby and they help us with childcare. When we are not working, we like to spend as much time as we can with our daughter Emma.'

financial help towards the costs of childcare for low-income families but daycare places are limited and waiting lists long. Also, there are regional differences. One recent effort by the government to help in this area has been the extension of paid maternity leave to one full year.

The 'sandwich generation'

The 'sandwich generation' is a nickname given to the group of people who are responsible for taking care of their children as well as their ageing parents. It is estimated that over two million people between the ages of 30 and 59 are providing home care to an elderly family member. This includes taking them to appointments, providing meals and checking on their well-being. Much of the responsibility for caring still falls on women. Some are forced into choosing between following a career and caring for a family.

Changing diets

Many Canadians lead very busy lives and eating habits are changing as a result. Fast-food shops flourish on many street corners. Here people of all ages can be seen eating a hurried meal instead of cooking for themselves. Grocery stores stock frozen meals and ready-prepared foods so that customers can eat quickly and easily at home.

Even the traditional Thanksgiving celebration is changing. Canadians celebrate Thanksgiving in October. During this time, families make a special effort to be together and cook a traditional meal of roast turkey, cranberry sauce, squash, stuffing and potatoes. The usual dessert is pumpkin pie.

▶ *A takeaway selling Middle Eastern specialities for people in a hurry.*

IN THEIR OWN WORDS

'Hi, I'm Tanya Taylor and I've worked in a doughnut shop for about three years. Before that, I was at university studying to be a nurse but I decided to take time off education – this is something that a lot of young people in Canada do. Now that I've experienced a little of life, I'll go back to university next year. This chain of doughnut shops was set up 35 years ago – now there are over 2,200 shops throughout Canada. We sell over 40 different types of doughnut and some of our stores are open 24 hours a day. It's a great place for people to bring their kids, or meet their friends.'

In the past it was common for an extended family to gather at one house to share this harvest meal. While some families still do this, the gatherings are often much smaller today. Some people prefer to meet at a restaurant for their Thanksgiving meal.

Because Canada's population is so diverse, different families have different staple foods. Improvements in transport and food preservation mean that foods can be flown in from all over the world, and people can enjoy the traditional dishes of many different cultures. Soya sauce, salsa, ketchup and wasabi can all be found in the same store (or the same shopping trolley!). In the far north, people's diets used to be limited to what they could catch by hunting or fishing. Improvements in transport mean that a much greater variety of food can now be brought in.

◀ A Chinese supermarket in Toronto's Chinatown.

Leisure

Most people think of Canadians as 'outdoors people' and many do spend their leisure time skiing, skating or snowboarding in the winter. Snowmobiles were invented to help people get around in isolated communities, but now riding snowmobiles is a popular leisure activity. The winters in many parts of Canada are long, cold and dark so winter sports are a great way to get some exercise and enjoy some fresh air.

▲ *Skiing has been a popular pastime for many years.*

IN THEIR OWN WORDS

'Hi, I'm Tom Songhurst. I'm 20 and I'm from Bognor in the UK. I'm taking a year off university to see a bit of the world. Canada is a great place for outdoor activity. Right now, I'm enjoying a morning of mountain biking on this great trail but there is also rock climbing, canoeing and hiking.

'If I'm still here in the winter, I'll be going skiing and snowboarding – maybe even skating on the Rideau Canal in Ottawa. The scenery is amazing and so different from place to place. When the ice-hockey season starts I'd like to see a NHL match between the Toronto Maple Leafs and the Montréal Canadiens – there's quite a rivalry between them so it should be fun to watch. Maybe I'll even have a go at ice-hockey myself!'

During the rest of the year, other leisure activities compete for the time of Canadians. Roller-blading, riding scooters, singing in karaoke bars and salsa-dancing are popular pastimes. Children enjoy their computer games indoors and play in soccer, baseball and even lacrosse leagues when the weather permits. As the population ages, gardening at home has also become an increasingly popular hobby. Some people grow fruit and vegetables but many just enjoy the loveliness of a colourful garden.

Canada is also a place where foreign visitors come to spend their leisure time. Visitors from the USA find it less expensive to buy cottages in Canada than in many parts of their own country. They may come for fishing, white-water rafting or camping. On the east coast, tourists, especially from Japan, are eager to visit the places described in the popular *Anne of Green Gables* children's books, such as Prince Edward Island. The Calgary Stampede, an annual event in Alberta, attracts visitors from all over the world. This celebration of rodeo skills such as steer-wrestling and calf-roping began in 1912 and now lasts for ten days each year.

▼ *This group of tourists is setting off from Vancouver Island on a whale-watching trip.*

Healthcare

The healthcare system in Canada is based on the idea that everyone should have access to healthcare when they need it. People pay for health services through their taxes, rather than every time they visit a doctor or go into hospital. Generally, Canadians enjoy some of the best healthcare in the world but the type of healthcare they get does depend on where they live. In large cities such as Vancouver, Calgary, Winnipeg, Toronto and Montréal, there are modern, well-equipped hospitals. However, in more remote parts of Canada, people may have to drive for many hours to reach their nearest doctor.

As the population of Canada ages, the demand for healthcare and the cost of providing it rises. This is because elderly people tend to need more healthcare than younger people. Provincial governments are trying to change the way

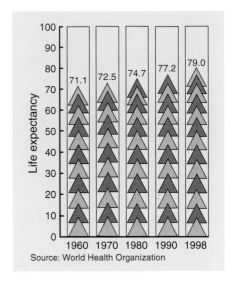

Source: World Health Organization

▲ Improvements in healthcare have contributed to increased life expectancy in Canada.

▲ Air ambulances like this one are used to transport people from remote areas to large hospitals for treatment.

IN THEIR OWN WORDS

'I'm Monica Lancaster and I'm a nurse practitioner. The introduction of nurse practitioners is one of the major changes that is occurring in healthcare in Canada. The nurse practitioner is a special type of nurse who has taken further training. This training allows us to diagnose certain illnesses, order some tests and prescribe appropriate medication. We usually work closely with doctors.

'New technology and improvements in medicines mean that we can successfully treat many more people these days. But new treatments and techniques can be very expensive – it puts a big strain on the healthcare system. There are shortages of certain types of doctor, too. The hope is that nurse practitioners will help to solve some of the problems caused by a shortage of family doctors in Canada.'

healthcare is provided. They are encouraging family doctors and other health workers, such as nurse practitioners, to provide a wider range of treatments in the local community. The aim is to reduce the number of patients who have to be treated in hospitals. They are also trying to change the way doctors are paid. They want doctors to be paid a fixed salary for treating a specific group of patients, instead of being paid a fee for each patient they treat. They hope that this will reduce costs, but not all doctors support the idea.

▶ *Telecommunications play an important role in Canadian healthcare. People living in remote areas can call nurses and doctors to ask for advice.*

Education

Canadian children generally go to school for about 6.5 hours a day, five days per week. Primary and secondary schooling is free to all families. Some parents, however, choose to pay to send their children to private schools – perhaps because of religious beliefs or because the class sizes are smaller. Parents also have the right to teach their own children themselves at home, as long as they comply with certain rules.

College and university education is subsidized by the government but is not free. In recent years, it has become more and more expensive for families to send their children to university. Some people are concerned that if this trend continues, a university degree may become a

▲ *Children boarding the bus to school in Manitoba. Children living in remote areas have a long journey to school each day.*

◄ *University students in Toronto. The number of people in Canada who have university degrees is increasing – up from around 6 per cent in the mid-1970s to approximately 15 per cent today.*

IN THEIR OWN WORDS

'Hi, we're Michael, Daniel, Laura, Carina and Benjamin. We attended the same elementary school together for about ten years. Now that we are 14 and in grade 9, some of us have chosen different high schools. There are all-boy schools, all-girl schools and co-ed schools. We decide with our parents which school would be best for us.

'We all wear uniforms to school but some of our friends don't. Some schools let you wear what you want. It used to be that only private schools had uniforms but now all types of schools have them.'

privilege only the wealthy can afford. There are some schemes such as scholarships and government loans to help cover the costs of higher education but many students leave university with debts of thousands of dollars.

Arguments over education

Education in Canada is under the control of provincial governments but local school boards have a lot of freedom to decide how schools in their areas should be run. For example, some schools, especially in cities, have a lot of pupils whose first language is neither English nor French. The school boards in these areas have to set aside money to pay for specialist language teachers and for translators, so that the school can communicate properly with pupils' families. Schools in rural areas have different issues to deal with. Now, however, some provincial governments want to reduce the amount of freedom local school boards have. Teachers' groups have opposed the changes over several years and there have been many strikes.

Farming and fishing

In the past many Canadians worked in farming and fishing but today less than 3 per cent of the population earn their living this way. It is often difficult for small farms to compete with large ones, so farms have tended to merge and the number of farm-owners has fallen. New technology has helped to make farming and fishing more efficient, but often it also means that fewer workers are needed. For example, most dairy farms use milking machines that can be operated by just a few workers, rather than milking a herd of cows by hand. The younger generation may decide not to follow in their parents' footsteps, so the future of a family farm is threatened.

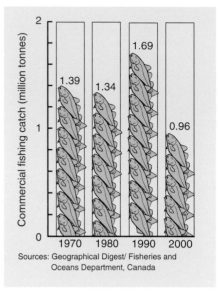

Sources: Geographical Digest/ Fisheries and Oceans Department, Canada

▲ *Fishing catches almost halved over the ten years to 2000, as fish stocks collapsed and strict limits were put on catches.*

◀ *Fishing boats tied up and lying idle at Nanaimo on Vancouver Island. Overfishing has led to a decline in the number of people who make their living this way.*

IN THEIR OWN WORDS

'I'm Annie Kulyk. My parents came to Canada from the Ukraine in 1914 and I was born two years later. I was one of three children, but my father died when I was two years old and my mother was left alone in a foreign land. In those days, there were a lot of Ukrainians in this part of Canada, so my mother soon married another Ukrainian man and had five more children. Because I was the oldest girl I was in charge of babysitting and cooking for our household. In those days, we had no electricity and I cooked on an open fire until 1945! Farming was tough too with few machines to help us. Later, my husband taught me how to drive a tractor and last fall I ploughed 20 acres just to prove to my grandson that his grandmother still had it in her!'

Specialized businesses

Some farmers have turned to specialized businesses in order to survive. They may have found, for example, that they can make more profits by growing ginseng, or producing ostrich meat for the gourmet market, than by growing potatoes. Organic farming is another area that is developing. Some people are concerned about possible health risks and the damage to the environment linked to intensive farming. They are willing to pay more for fruit, vegetables and meat that have been produced without the use of chemicals. Businesses that allow farms to sell direct to specific families or that deliver fresh produce are flourishing.

Fishermen have looked for other ways to boost their income too. Some run fishing trips for people who fish for sport rather than as a job. Others take tourists on sightseeing trips.

▼ *Ginseng is an important ingredient in Chinese medicines and other herbal remedies. Growing this crop has provided farmers with a new source of income.*

Manufacturing

Manufacturing employs many Canadians, producing goods for sale at home and abroad. Although the percentage of the population working in manufacturing has declined slightly since the late 1980s, to under 15 per cent today, this is still a significant number of citizens. However, with the use of more computer-based technology the number is expected to continue to decrease. In the past, people could expect to stay in a manufacturing job for their entire working life. Now the type of products people want to buy and the technology used to make them change much more quickly than they used to, so manufacturing jobs are not as secure as they used to be.

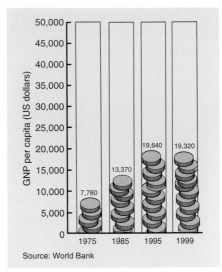

Source: World Bank

▲ Canada's income from the goods and services it produces has almost trebled since 1975.

◄ Paper is an important product of Canada's industries. This mill produces pulp from wood, and the pulp is then made into paper.

The manufacture of vehicles and other transport equipment is especially important to the Canadian economy. One company that was first set up in a garage in a small village in Québec found a big market for innovative products such as its snowmobile, and is now an industry leader in North America and parts of Europe. Canadians are proudest of their contribution to space research. Canadian ingenuity

IN THEIR OWN WORDS

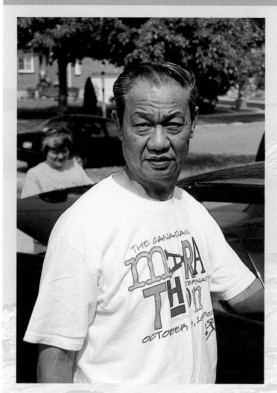

'I'm Eugene Li. My wife, Rose, and I both work in the manufacturing sector. When I first arrived from India in 1972, I found a job as a tool-and-die maker at a company that manufactured parts for aeroplanes. My wife and two children stayed in Calcutta and joined me two years later. By then, I had saved enough to buy a condominium unit.

'I have four children. Three of them have university degrees and the youngest has just started high school. They will not work in manufacturing because the security is no longer there and the reason we came to Canada was to give our children a better life. We hope they will become professionals – the eldest is a teacher. However, my job has given me and my family a decent lifestyle and now Rose and I are looking forward to retirement. I'm looking forward to devoting more time to training for the marathon runs I take part in every year.'

and technology have produced the Mobile Servicing System, which is also known as Canadarm 2. This clever device is essential to the completion of the International Space Station.

One advantage Canadians enjoy in manufacturing is that the United States dollar has a higher value than the Canadian dollar. Many Canadian manufacturers make products for the US market because it is cheaper for the US company to have goods produced in Canada. When the exchange rate is considered, the Americans are getting a real bargain!

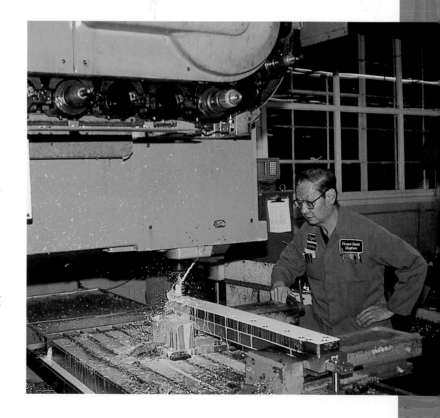

▶ *Mr Li (see above) at work on the production line, where parts for aircraft are manufactured.*

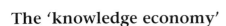
The 'knowledge economy'

Today, most young people look for a career outside the traditional sectors of farming, fishing and manufacturing. There has been a big movement towards jobs that generate ideas or provide expert advice. These are referred to as the 'knowledge economy'. Jobs like these need a well-educated workforce and the government stresses the importance of education, including literacy, mathematics, science and information technology.

◀ *Developments in information technology have meant that workers have the freedom to work when they want, where they want.*

Small businesses

An increasing number of people are setting up their own businesses and working from their homes or renting small offices. Such businesses may include website design, financial advising, or freelance writing. Technological developments mean that people no longer have to spend time every day commuting to a city office. They can choose to live in rural areas, where houses are cheaper and the local environment is

IN THEIR OWN WORDS

'I'm Neil Jenkins. I'm 20 years old and studying Management and Economics at university. Right now I work part-time for a big computer company where my father worked for over 25 years. I'd be happy to have a job like his but I'm not sure if such secure jobs will be around in the future. I think people will have to get used to working in different sorts of job as the economy changes. I operated an internet radio station for about a year but was asked to stop because regulations have been brought in to govern that type of activity. I started to teach myself website design too but technology seems to be advancing far too quickly to work at these things as a hobby. There are great opportunities within the knowledge economy but proper training is essential.'

more pleasant. They can work on a computer at home and use the internet to communicate with colleagues. The number of Canadians with access to the internet at home leapt by 12 per cent between 1997 and 1999.

This kind of working life is attracting young people and those looking for a change in mid-life. They no longer have the security of knowing that they will get a regular pay cheque but they have more freedom to work in the way they choose. If their businesses grow, they may be able to employ other people.

▶ *Fifteen-year-old Matthew Schaffer has a weekend job at his parents' petrol station but when he leaves school he would like to be a graphic designer, with his own studio.*

9 The Way Ahead

Canadians are generally optimistic about the future. With a high standard of living, good education and excellent healthcare, they have much to be thankful for. However, the nation does face many challenges. There is still debate, for example, about how to get the right balance between the powers of the federal government and the powers of provincial governments.

◀ *A banner stretches across a road in British Columbia. It is protesting against tourist development in the traditional homeland of native Canadians.*

The establishment of Nunavut in the north is one example of how the government has dealt with the demands of native Canadians to better land rights. Other groups of native Canadians are still calling for their rights to be recognized. Debates continue over whether Québec will remain part of Canada and over the language rights of French Canadians. These matters will continue to challenge Canadians as the country continues to grow. Canada, though, has a good history of being able to reach consensus, which helps to strengthen the national identity.

IN THEIR OWN WORDS

'Hi, I'm Melanie MacMillan. I've been flying for six years and I'm a commercial pilot. I joined a small, new airline when it was set up in 2001 and we fly people from the international airport in Vancouver to Vancouver Island – 'across the puddle', as we say out here.

'I love flying and Canada is a fantastic place to work. There are more light commercial aircraft in Canada than in any other country in the world and lots of them land and take off from the sea or the thousands of lakes. These are called float planes and I hope to get my licence to fly them very soon. The sky's the limit in Canada and I'm ready to take off!'

Although Canadians come from many parts of the world, they share an appreciation of the freedoms enjoyed by all. As the children grow and learn to live together in increasing harmony, the country grows stronger.

▼ *Canadians make the most of their country's wonderful landscape and clean environment.*

Glossary

Atlantic provinces Nova Scotia, New Brunswick, Prince Edward Island, Newfoundland and the Labrador region.

Biomass Wood and vegetable waste.

Co-ed school A co-educational school, in which boys and girls are taught together.

Condominium unit An apartment within an apartment block.

Constitution The laws that set out how a country is to be governed.

Deciduous Losing all leaves every year at the end of the growing season.

Dominion A country that has its own government but is part of a larger grouping of countries. Canada was a dominion of the British Empire.

Drought A long period with very little or no rain.

Elementary school Primary school.

Exports Goods that are sold to other countries.

Federal government The central government of a country that is divided up into provinces. It deals with issues affecting the country as a whole, such as defence.

GNP per capita GNP is gross national product, the total value of goods and services produced by a country each year, including investments in the country by other nations. Per capita means per person, so GNP per capita is the total value of goods, etc., divided by the total population.

Gross domestic product The total value of the goods and services produced by a country each year.

Head of state The person at the head of a nation. The British monarch is head of state in several countries that used to be part of the British Empire, but the countries are run by their elected governments.

Hydroelectricity Electricity that is generated from turbines turned by the force of falling water.

Immigrants People who come to live in a country.

Inuktitut The Inuit language.

Jetski A craft like a motorbike that is used in water sports. It carries one or two people and can go very fast.

Longliner A fisherman who fishes in deep water for large quantities of fish, using a long line with several shorter hooks attached to it.

Lumber Logs of wood.

Maternity leave Time off work before and after the birth of a baby.

Organic farming Farming without the use of chemicals such as artificial fertilizers, or products to make animals grow faster.

Photochemical smog Air pollution produced when sunlight reacts with chemicals in, for example, car exhaust.

Prairie A flat, treeless, grassy landscape in the United States and Canada.

Precipitation Moisture in the atmosphere that falls as rain, snow, hail or sleet.

Provincial government The government of a province (a large region of a country). It deals with issues affecting the region, such as jobs.

Ratify To formally approve an agreement.

Referendum A vote on a specific issue.

Refugees People who have left their homes or their home country because they fear their lives are in danger, as a result of war, natural disaster or because of their political or religious beliefs.

Rodeo A display of cowboy skills.

Shingles Roof tiles.

Snowmobile A small vehicle designed to transport one or two people over snow and ice.

Sponsor To agree to provide support for a period of ten years for a relative who wants to come to live in Canada. The aim is to ensure that immigrants coming to join their families do not have to ask for financial help from the Canadian government.

Staple foods The basic foods that make up a person's diet, such as bread or rice.

Subsidized Partially paid for.

Thanksgiving A celebration that originally marked the first harvest gathered in by the first European settlers in North America.

Uranium A metal that is used as a source of nuclear energy.

Further Information

Books to read

The Kids' Book of Canada by Barbara Greenwood (Kids Can Press, Toronto, 1999)

Wow Canada! Exploring this land from coast to coast to coast by Vivien Bowers (Maple Tree Press, 1999)

Visit to Canada by Mary Quigley (Heinemann Library, 2003)

Websites

www.climatechange.gc.ca/info
This site run by the Canadian government focuses on climate change and environmental initiatives around the country.

www.canada.gc.ca
This is the main government website with information about the country and how it is run, plus topics such as health, jobs, etc.

www.canadaplace.gc.ca
This site provides information about Canada's history as well as current affairs and an index of online newspapers. It has categories aimed specifically at young people.

www.statcan.ca
This site provides a wide range of useful statistics on various topics such as families, work, population, etc.

The website addresses (URLs) included in this book were valid at the time of going to press. However, because of the nature of the Internet, it is possible that some addresses may have changed, or sites may have changed or closed down since publication. While the authors and Publishers regret any inconvenience this may cause the readers, no responsibility for any such changes can be accepted by either the author or the Publisher.

Index

Page numbers in **bold** refer to photographs, maps or statistics panels.